MOETIVATION

THIS BOOK IS DEDICATED TO
MY CHILDHOOD SOFTBALL COACH
MR. JASON REED

A True Love Story to Self

Thank you for Your Support!

Part I

The chances you take, the people you meet, the people you love, the faith you have That's what's going to define you

-Denzel Washington

Once again, I've fallen flat on my face because of my mouth. Yesterday I lost my job of eight years. I'm currently in love with a woman named Ms. Cleveland who is addicted to penis, cocaine, and me giving her head. To top it all off, my best friend is kicking me out after I gave her all my money for bills.

How many times have I been there?

I should do everyone a favor and run my car into the closest brick wall. Funny thing is, it's not my car. It's my mother's. She'd kill me if I hurt her car.

> *"When are you going to get it together, Monichia?"*
> *"You lose everything behind these women."*
> *"You have to call your momma."*

Checks Banking App: **Available balance $1.42**

I dug into my pockets and pulled out a crisp five-dollar bill and in the corner, I had a big jar filled with a lot of coins. I sat on the floor and contemplated spending that five dollars on a four for four at Wendy's or a pack of cigarettes. I chose the cigarettes.

My mother was on her honeymoon when I called. The phone call cut me to my core. I hated the fact that I was her only disappointment. I know she was probably telling her new husband how awesome her Moe Moe is. Now my awesome overgrown ass has to come live with them.

Damn.

I live inside a box that is 80 inches long, 30 inches wide, and
30 inches deep. I call this box "House." Inside of House are
[handwritten: Foundation]
a lot of bubbles. These bubbles represent life and how I deal
with it. Sometimes I pop them as they form, and other times
I find it hard to keep up. The recurring bubbles—*RENT,
ATTENTION, DEPRESSION, CRAMPS, HUNGER*—come
in House way too often. Too many bubbles have imbedded
themselves into the cellular structure of House. Those
bubbles hurt the most.

At the top of House is a battery meter. It measures
the percentage of control I have on my reality. I'm currently
reading **17%**. I do not remember my meter ever reading
anything higher than **50%**. It seems as though every time I
have reached for a higher elevation more bubbles appeared,
and eventually I lost control of House. [handwritten: My foundation crumbles.]

At the bottom of House are six tubes. Within each of
these tubes are wires that connect me to everyone in my
world. I had to learn that everyone connected to me through
my wires affects me in some form. They add to my charge or
take away from it. My tubes represent my functions; they
were heavy, but are clean now. I've replaced two since my
mother had to come rescue me.

[handwritten: withdraw or deposit into my em Bank]

That night, I was reading **4%**. Five out of the six tubes connected to House had self-destructed. There was not even a chair for me to sit on at the bottom. I just laid there and let the bubbles have their way with me.

My Sexual Tube contained over 100 wires connected to over 100 different women. The tube had burst open from reaching its maximum capacity. Sixty-five percent of the wires in my Sexual Tube were also connected to me through my Financial Tube, Emotional Tube, Physical Tube, and Mental Tube.

My Financial Tube had several wires burning inside of it. The tube had holes throughout its length from the flames, leaving the majority of the wires insufficient. The wire in this tube that was connected to my mother had been burned out and replaced on many occasions. These were instances when she would rip her wire out of my tube. And a short time later, House would crumble. The dysfunctions of the tube made it impossible to pop a *RENT* bubble in Atlanta, so I had nowhere to go.

My Physical Tube had rust throughout it, and the tube itself had disconnected from House. Toxins ate through each wire, causing the tube many malfunctions. It was filled with everything that wasn't healthy but made me feel better. The tube simply got too heavy. I didn't even notice I gained the weight, but once I did it was too late and the tube just fell off.

My Emotional Tube was filled with wires that were covered in mildew. Sparks flickered throughout the tube. Its walls were painted with tears and aches of past lovers my heart couldn't let go of. Its wires ran deep with pain into House's core, causing those same wires to bud out into my Mental Tube.

My Mental Tube was smut black. The smoke sent steady vibrations throughout the tube. The mildew from my Emotional Tube had spread through the wires in my Mental Tube, causing complete disarray. Any decisions made weren't processed correctly, ultimately leading to the wrong one. When the sparks spread throughout the tube, the echoes followed. Irrational decisions mixed with the smoke meant pure destruction.

My Spiritual Tube was the only one clean and flowing. It had two wires. One connected to my grandmother and the other to my mother. That night it was their prayers that gave me my last **4%**.

I consider myself a crayon I might not
be your favorite color, but one day
you're going to need me to complete
your picture
-Lauryn Hill

May 30, 2016   **Current Reading: 19%**

I laid under the quilted bedspread in my mother's guest
room. She lived in Valdosta, Georgia. What I call the
country. I had to get out of there. What I hated the most was
every time I wanted to smoke a cigarette the damn door
would snitch on me.

> *"FRONT door!"*
> *"BACK door!"*

I felt like they were clocking my moves. It was time
to go. That night I wrote down everything I needed to do.
The mission was to live a life where I didn't have to depend
on anyone. I had to devise a plan to take over the world and
be the one to change it. I didn't know how to get something
like this done, but being positive, I felt, was the best place to
start. By thinking positive, doing positive things, and
choosing a positive outcome, I figured positive vibes would
be returned. I had to be creative to motivate myself. I wanted
to be the Burj Khalifa, the tallest building in the world. I
wanted to be just as tall.

Now the bottom was relaxing. There were less
bubbles in House while I was living in my mother's home.
However, I was ready for the bubbles, ready to be stable. I

was honestly just ready to come up out of the guest bathroom.

So, I thought up The 30-Day Challenge. Everything that needed to be done would become a goal. Once I completed a goal, I would replace it with three new ones. The official start date to my challenge was June 01, 2016, and my first three goals were:

-Sign my own lease
-Lose 50 pounds
-Get a promotion

Plan your Work

Work your Plan

-Mr. Jones

10th Grade Science Teacher

"Get a promotion" - Completed

I had taken the test for this promotion in Atlanta three times. I failed every time. Because I was in a new city, I had to get new results. I walked into the conference room claiming the promotion. You had a front-of-the-house test, and a back-of-the-house test. I took both. I passed both. The plan was in progress. It was time to elevate.

New Goals

-Feed the Homeless

-Donate Blood

-Do something kind for a stranger

Ambition is a Dream, with a V8 engine

-Elvis Presley

"Sign my own lease" - Completed

When I made my request, I wasn't being greedy. I just asked for what I needed. I asked for a cheap, one bedroom, one bathroom, total electric, with a washer/dryer hookup. I ended up with a college-style student setup. I had roommates, and we shared the kitchen, living room, pretty much everything outside of my bedroom and my bathroom. It came furnished, it had a washer and dryer, and a balcony to smoke on.

Man, you couldn't tell me nothing. I could not wait to invite a little cutie over. Cook a little something and put a little pressure between her ears. I was feeling like Moe again in my little bed and bath. Ready to take someone's daughter beyond. Ready for bubbles, and everything coming behind it.

My rent was $399, with the cable and Wi-Fi included. I was finally winning.

New Goals

-Earn my wings

-Travel on a plane state to state

-Visit The Ellen Show

Be Kind to One Another

-Ellen DeGeneres

"Do something kind for a stranger" – Completed

I must be the only person in the world whose *RENT* bubble is $399 and I can't pop it. When it floated into House, I just put my head down. I was $16 short. $16. I can't ask my momma for no funky $16.

How did I get here, right? Especially after the promotion? Well, I had a bright idea. Since I buy cigarettes every day, I could do something kind every day for a stranger. The value was $5 because that's how much a pack cost. The month of June had 30 days, so I picked 30 strangers. I told myself if I didn't smoke then I could be nice to people. Give people a smile and make their day brighter. Well, I started smoking again by Day 6, but I continued to be nice to people.

"I paid for three of my customers' food at work."

"I randomly drove in drive-thrus and paid for the person's food behind me 10 times."

"I over-tipped a bartender."

"I purchased four lottery tickets valued at $5."

"I gave six homeless men $5."

"I won a little girl a bear out of the claw machine at work."

"I purchased three strangers' favorite chips and drink at the corner store."

"At that same store, I put an additional $5 in two strangers' gas tanks."

Now the rent is due in my new place, and I don't have the whole amount. Luckily for me my winner from Day 5, the bartender, spotted me $20. Even though I got carried away with the giving, because it ended up being expensive, I was truly dedicated to my challenge. It felt good being kind. I enjoyed being positive. Some days were hard, but I made it my purpose to make other people smile. It was my duty.

Checks Banking App: **Available balance $0.09**

New Goals

-Walk in Las Vegas, Nevada

-Walk in California

-Walk in Australia

September 7, 2016   **Current Reading: 20%**

"Earn my wings" - Completed

I was only getting scheduled 12 hours at my home store. I felt like my boss hated me, so I applied for a promotion to get out of her store. She lost my application twice. Determined to not let her ruin my chance, I sent the application in myself. Attached was an email letting them know I was ready and needed to know what to do.

It was a Wednesday, and I was sitting on the beach in Jacksonville, Florida, when I got the phone call. It was my future boss calling to see when we could schedule an interview. I told him there was no better time than now. Especially while I was laying out in the sun. I blew him clean out of the water. He promoted me during the interview to a team that assisted in new restaurant openings across the country. I wanted that promotion so bad that I became the promotion. Don't know how to explain it. I just knew I had to become everything I needed to be. So that day I told myself, "I am the brand. Now act accordingly."

New Goals

-Learn to Swim

-Learn to Fish

-Learn to Walk in Heels

You need a little bit of Insanity to do

Great Things

-Henry Rollins

October 7, 2016   **Current Reading: 18%**

"Travel by plane from state to state" - Completed

I got my first assignment, and it was in Iowa. My first time on a plane, and they sent me to Iowa. Apparently, the team and I were there to clean up and reopen restaurants. If they needed me to scrub toilets with a toothbrush, I would've done it with a smile. It didn't matter where they sent me or what they needed done; I wasn't leaving until the job was complete.

Checks Banking App: **Available balance $6.38**

I must be crazy or dumb, but I had to go. My mother paid for my bag to get checked in. She gave me a look that meant don't ask for anything else. I needed so much, though. If she only knew how terrified I was to get on that plane. I did not want to die. But if I died trying, then that would be okay. When I landed, I checked my pocket. I had $20, and I was starving.

New Goals

-**Save $50**

-**Raise Credit Score by 50 points**

-**No alcohol for seven days**

Failure is simply the opportunity to begin again, this time more intelligently

Henry Ford

Checks Banking App: **Available balance –$2.85**

The bubbles were taking over. The company said
they would give me $20 a day for food and other things I
needed. I'd been in Iowa for 16 days and hadn't received
any money yet. Apparently, because I was new to the team,
nothing had been fully processed. Hell, I came here with
nothing and now I'm negative nothing. I hadn't gotten
waxed since I left home, so I was practically growing a
whole beard. I hadn't had a haircut, and I know my
eyebrows looked a mess.

I got up from my hotel bed, and as soon as I looked
in the mirror, the bubble came—*UGLY*. I was angry to see it.
No matter how much I hated it, I couldn't pop it. It floated
right past me and sat in its normal corner. I started crying
when *CRAMPS* came floating in, and right behind it was
AUNTIE FLO. I didn't even have any soap. I was using the
hotel bar. I wasn't equipped to deal with any bubbles, and
here they came in a pack. I remember my mother saying she
put tampons in my bag, just in case. I ran to it. There were
only three. Three tampons to get me through the next five

days. I closed my eyes. I could hear more bubbles coming. *PAIN, DEPRESSION, LONELINESS, ANXIETY, HUNGER.*

I didn't have anyone to call. I honestly forgot why I was there. I didn't know what part of the plan this was. I could've been broke at home. At least I could go to my mother's and eat. I was starving. And my boss wasn't answering the phone. I couldn't ask Ms. Valdosta or my momma for more money.

Later that day, I had a mental breakdown. Once the sparks and echoes started in my Mental Tube, I became a hazard. When my Mental Tube turned black, my next move wouldn't be my best. My teammates caught me that day, and brought me back to reality. The ladies got together and purchased soap, tampons, shampoo, conditioner, razors, shaving cream, and face scrub. I wasn't embarrassed at all. I needed everything. I needed them. In that moment, I knew I was part of a family and I would be okay; but I still needed my money.

Current Reading: 14%

October 26, 2016   **Current Reading: 28%**

"Walk in California" - Completed

Checks Banking App: **Available balance $1,378.47**

I received another assignment while already being on one. They were sending me to San Francisco, California. SAN FRANCISCO! This time it's an actual opening. So now I am officially a trainer assisting in the opening of a brand-new restaurant. The airline was Southwest. It was the most beautiful plane I had ever seen. It was huge. It had three sections, with three columns per section, and three chairs per row. I was amazed. My seat was in the very back. Nobody was back there but me and two other people. I felt damn good. When the flight attendant came with her little phone, I was sitting at attention. She smiled and said my total was $142.

I had four sandwiches, four Pringles (I got every variety box), beer, and some Jack. I was sitting pretty and enjoying the view.

New Goals

-Complete a New Restaurant Opening

-Go to the strip club for first time

-Build a Kite

For every dark night there's a brighter

day

-Tupac

**"Complete one new restaurant opening" -
Completed**

The plane ride back to Georgia was the longest. I sat in the middle seat in the last row, right by the bathroom. I couldn't sleep on my five-hour ride, so I went to my Goals book and looked over the plan. I felt good about my first opening. It really seemed like the team loved me. I was on a trip with the best of the best, literally five of them were among the top ten performers. I had the Cream of the Crop right here before me. Therefore, I just politely took a seat at the table and watched carefully. I noticed that no one on the trip, whether they were good or not, took this opportunity as seriously as I did, so in my heart I knew this takeover would be fun. My mentor and roommate for this assignment was Ms. Chicago, and she was everything. To have her immediately plug into my Spiritual Tube was truly a blessing. I was on a mission. When you're introduced to the best, you adapt and exceed. There is a plan in full effect, and I had to remain focused. Of course, I had fun. But the goal was to be number one.

The only way this will work is if I become an asset. I wanted them to need me, so I can stay out of my home store. I couldn't go back there. So, I had to play, and my chips were all-in. I had a few bubbles floating, but they weren't anything I couldn't pop or keep at bay.

I felt good about coming home. I had been gone over a month now. My first time out the gate was a success. I told my mother I was buying Thanksgiving dinner. I caught up on my bills, and paid the $500 on my storage so they won't auction my things. I got a few new shirts and I bought some shoes from Target.

As soon as we landed, Checks Banking App: **Available balance $1,109.54.** Let's make this count.

New Goals

-Bring Less Moe to work and More Monichia

-Obtain a Passport

-Move Back to Atlanta

Yesterday the team had a conference call. There were about forty of us on the call. Guess who got a shout-out? Me! Apparently, my boss had received an email about my work ethic from the managers in Iowa, as well as an email from owners of the restaurant in California. My boss said all the owners' friends loved my attitude during the VIP and praised me for being the spotlight of the show. Needless to say, I was back on a plane in less than a week headed to Mount Sterling, Kentucky.

Guess who was my roommate? Ms. Chicago. She was absolutely brilliant. I told her she was my best friend and there was nothing she could do about it. This assignment was my second official opening, and I knocked it out of the park. I was cute the whole time with clear short nails and eye shadow. The acrylic nails were new for me, but I liked them. I'm in corporate now. So I needed to play the part.

New Goals

-Jump out a plane
-Purchase Land
-Take my mother on vacation

We have to teach our girls that they

can reach as high as Humanly Possible

-Beyoncé

A month later, I was still on the road. Somehow, I convinced my boss that I was ready to do a solo assignment. I was executing the plan flawlessly, and no one was even aware. This was my fourth assignment in three months, and I still had not returned to my home store. They sent me straight to Goodland, Kansas, from Kentucky to help a restaurant over the holidays. Because it was Christmas, I treated myself to a movie in Denver, Colorado. I drove through my first snowstorm that day. I cried through every minute of it, but the adrenaline from the experience did my soul good. My Christmas dinner was a burger at a truck stop. My double was fresh off the broiler, and my fries were piping hot. I was truly living my best life.

I am where I am because I believe in
all possibilities
-Whoopi Goldberg

When it happened, I was alone in my hotel room in Goodland, Kansas. I was sure I had lost my mind, but the image of her was so clear. She had my face, but I knew my mother would have told me if I had a twin. She stood there in red pumps with a matching pants suit. Her red lips were perfect. I was so confused. How did she get into my hotel room? I was too scared to ask.

I nervously said, "Hello."

She smiled, and my heart eased. "How are you, Monichia? Please don't be alarmed. There's no need to because, well, I'm you."

I looked her up and down. "I can see that," I replied, "but, really, who are you and what are you doing here?"

She wasn't me at all. She had my face, but she was gorgeous. Her hair, in a tight ponytail, laid down her back. Her teeth were picture-perfect white with no gap in the middle. Her gums were even pink. She had a small waist with nice hips, and her butt sat up a lot higher than mine.

"I'm your conscience, Monichia." She smiled again. "You don't remember me? My name is Monroe Star."

That is when it finally started to make sense. Monroe was my best friend when I was a little girl. She was there for me those nights when I would slice my thighs. She even taught me how to clean my wounds with peroxide. We ate lunch together in the bathroom when I was too afraid to go into the cafeteria with my peers. She was there beside me every day telling me to "Ignore them," "Keep walking," "Don't cry," "Run," "You're not ugly."

It had been years since I had seen her. I was confused about her returning now—I'm an adult. "Why are you here?"

She sat down on the other queen-size bed and looked me over. "I see you've grown nicely. Nice nails. It seems as if you are coming into yourself as a woman."

I exhaled. "I really don't know what I'm doing, Monroe, but everyone seems to like it." She smiled. "But do you like it?"

I thought about it. "I guess. I like the attention. I posted a picture on social media on Christmas and got almost 200 likes. I've never had so many people give me so many compliments, especially on a picture."

"Again, do you like it, Monichia?"

I smiled and jumped up. "I do. I really, really do. I've never felt so pretty, Monroe." I started spinning around. "Do you remember back in the day when they called me three necks? Well, guess who's got two now?"

We laughed. I sat back down with a smile.

"Do you think you will be making this permanent?" Monroe asked.

"I don't know. It's kind of expensive being a girl."

With a smirk, she replied. "It's not expensive being a girl. What's expensive is you taking care of so many other women. When it's time to do for you, your pockets are empty."

"How do you know I've been taking care of other women? I haven't seen you since we left Valdosta when I was a little girl. You left me, Monroe. I called out to you night after night, and you never came."

She looked into my eyes. "Monichia, I never left you, but it was time for you to make new friends. Real ones." Monroe got up and walked toward the window. "I've been here the entire time."

Skeptical, I asked, "When?"

"I was there when you smoked your first joint. Remember you thought you were dying and couldn't breathe?" We both laughed. "I was with you every night you would sneak off and go drinking with your friends. You were only fourteen years old, popping ecstasy pills."

"I was terrified of your surroundings," she continued. I watched her gazing out the window. "You had put all your trust in them, and had no awareness of anything." She looked back at me. "I was there when you crashed. I sat with you in that cold cell. I was so happy when we got out."

"We?" I asked confused. "So why show yourself now? What do you want with me?"

She turned and sat down on the edge of the bed. "I'm here because you have to fulfill your destiny. You have finally reached 50%. Now it's time for me to dig." Monroe looked me in my eyes. "I'm here to dig for you."

"You're here to dig? Dig what?" I asked, laughing.

Patiently she asked, "How tall is the Burj Khalifa?"

I grabbed my phone to ask Siri. She replied, "The Burj Khalifa is 2,717 feet tall."

"Correct, and its concrete foundation is buried 164 feet deep. It would not be able to withstand its height on its own, so its foundation had to be dug deep into the earth for stability."

Still confused, I asked, "So while you're digging, what do I need to do?"

Monroe got up and walked toward the door. She looked back, smiled, and said, "Keep elevating, and when you're ready, write a love letter to yourself. Tell your heart what it needs to hear."

As the door closed behind her, I felt oddly a little violated, yet intrigued.

Step out of the history that is holding you back. Step into the new story you are willing to create

-Oprah Winfrey

Goals Completed

41. Visit 5 New States and Bring home a souvenir

14. Train grill at a New Restaurant Opening

171. Go to a professional Basketball game

Coming back home from Kansas felt liberating. I didn't fully understand what my destiny was; however, I was ready to do whatever it took for fulfillment. I was still on my original mission, which was to not depend on anyone but myself. Since it was a new year, I decided to create a new challenge. My Yearly Challenge. I would do my best to accomplish as many goals as I could in 365 days. I started 2017 with 264 goals, and planned to add more as the year continued.

This month I opened another restaurant in Locust Grove, Georgia. I had the pleasure of training grill for the first time, and it was a pure disaster. I honestly bit off more than I could chew. Once opening day was completed, embarrassed, I went back to my hotel room and cried for an hour. I had made up my mind that if they gave me another opportunity I would be flawless. The only thing positive about my failure was that there was nowhere to go but up. I wanted to be the best and that was the only option; so, I studied everything about grill before I left Locust Grove.

During the opening, my boss treated the team to an Atlanta Hawks home game. I was so excited to continue achieving my goals, and this one was fun. I had a great time, and Ms. Chicago was there as well. She wasn't my roommate this time, but it was good to have her in my presence.

Side note: I received a phone call from Ms. Cleveland. She finally returned my calls and ended up asking me to be the godmother to her unborn child. Of course, I said yes. Truth is, I was still in love with her, and would be willing to do whatever she needed or wanted me to do. It had been months since we actually talked so I wasn't sure how serious the proposal was but I had forgiven her for everything and was filled with nothing but support.

Goals Completed

31. Learn to fish

65. Obtain fishing License

131. Bring Less Moe and More Monichia to work

1. Obtain a passport

128. Babysit a Newborn

121. Pet a snake

124. Make a homemade pecan pie

18. Build a kite

56. Flirt with a random guy and get his number

Mini Challenge: Day 54 out 365
February 23, 2018
Complete 10 goals before Scandal *comes on.*

Before we get started, let's talk about how my team
won the Super Bowl. I don't know what Atlanta was
thinking, but everyone now knows who the real G.O.A.T. is.
I completed several goals this month. I started my mini
challenge at a lake in Valdosta, Georgia, with Ms. Willie and

her husband. They taught me how to bait a hook, cast it, and wait. I didn't catch anything that day. But I had a blast trying.

That afternoon I went to the store to get supplies to bake my first homemade pecan pie. You wouldn't believe it, but I purchased the wrong crust. I got a cake pan and lined it with the crust and made a deep-dish pecan pie. I don't care what anybody said, the pie was damn good. While shopping for my pecan pie ingredients, I ran into a couple with a snake and they let me touch it. The goal was to pet it, so I was happy we took care of that one. I am so terrified of snakes I almost pissed on myself when I touched it, but I did it.

In that same store while getting my fishing license, I saw a guy who worked there putting coolers on the shelf. I asked him for his number and he said he wanted to take me out for a snack. In my heart I knew he was slow. But his confidence was amazing. No, I didn't call him, but the goal was completed either way.

With all the positivity happening, the best part of February was going to Ohio. I had to open a restaurant in Cleveland. I trained grill again and completely smashed it. I was flawless in training and extremely proud of myself and my trainees. They held it down, and I will forever be grateful.

If you're wondering about me being in Cleveland, Ohio, and if that had any significance to Ms. Cleveland . . . yes, I was in her hometown. To bring you up to speed—no, she is not a lesbian, but when I met her I was intoxicated by her energy. She was so beautiful that all the men wanted her. So, I guess that is part of what made it special having her between my legs. The woman put me through so much, though. I am sure I'm numb to anything else she could possibly do to me. The woman has broken chairs over my head for no reason at all. No one I dealt with wanted her in my life, but I didn't know if I wanted my life if she wasn't in it. No matter the abuse she inflicted, I still had no desire to be with anyone else. So being in her hometown was doing my soul some good.

I walked the streets of Cleveland with tight pants, knee-high boots, and acrylic nails. I hollered at every beautiful woman I saw. Searching for her in their voices. I was prime-time fine, and I put on for her. I wasn't that 300-pound stud anymore. I wore more than sweatpants and T-shirts. I was in love with me for the first time in my life. I was proud of my curves and imperfections. I was giving Cleveland everything I had, and my heart smiled through every minute of it. For the first time in a long time, I felt her.

So, everything was all good. Cleveland was truly good to me, and the people there were amazing.

Goals Completed

164. Put feet in the Pacific Ocean

170. Train Fountain at a New Restaurant opening

162. Put feet in Atlantic Ocean

*Mini Challenge: Day 70 out of 365
March 11, 2017
Make 70 people smile today!

The month of March was filled with nothing but great vibes and beautiful women. Ms. Atlanta came down to Valdosta, Georgia, to spend a few days with me. We had a blast. I wanted to complete some goals, so we decided to take a trip to the beach in Jacksonville, Florida, and we ended up finishing our night at a carnival. On the ride home, Monroe appeared in the backseat. She had on a pink blouse with matching bangles, and her studded diamond earrings reflected off the mirror. I glanced over at Ms. Atlanta sleeping so peacefully. The fact that she even felt comfortable enough to do so with me driving across state lines made me even more protective of her. Looking out the window, Monroe asked, "Did you have fun?"

I looked in my rearview mirror to catch a glance of Monroe, but she wouldn't look at me.

"Yes, I had fun." I switched to a high lane to pass a black Malibu driving extremely slow.

"Are you in love?" Monroe asked. At that moment, I felt her eyes stabbing the back of my head.

"Why would you ask me something like that?"

Monroe leaned toward us. She looked Ms. Atlanta over. "So, you aren't going to try to sleep with her tonight?"

I didn't answer and was slightly annoyed by Monroe's remarks. Feeling my frustration, Monroe leaned back into her seat.

"You're acting like you don't try to sleep with all your friends, Monichia. I'm asking that this time you reconsider."

I switched to the middle lane and eased off the gas. "Why is she so special?" I asked.

Monroe put her hand on my shoulder. "You don't see it now, but you two will benefit each other more as friends in the future."

When I looked back in the rearview, Monroe was gone.

When we returned to my home, I gave Ms. Atlanta the bed and I took the floor and slept beside my

ATTENTION bubble. This was the only time I was comfortable about being in the friend zone, and because Ms. Atlanta was so dope I was happy with my decision. About a week later, I was on a plane headed back to California. I was being sent to Yucca Valley to open another restaurant. Guess who was my roommate? Ms. Chicago.

A few hours away was the city of Santa Monica, so I decided to take another trip to the beach. The energy was so smooth between me and Ms. Chicago that it felt amazing. I couldn't imagine anything better than to be riding alongside my new best friend. There were no judgments being passed. Just love, genuine love, and mutual respect between the two of us.

As for the opening, I thought it went extremely well. It was my first time training fountain, and my trainees were the realest in the building. They were amazing. All sixteen of them.

Nothing is Impossible Even the word itself says "I'm Possible"

-Audrey Hepburn

Goals Completed

38. Train Grill three times at New Restaurant Opening

75. Do Karaoke in Three States

> **Mini Challenge: Day 116 out of 365*
> *April 26, 2017*
> *Donate $100 to someone in need.*

In April, I ended up in Ohio again, which is always positive. Toledo this time. I really enjoyed myself on this assignment. I was at a university, and I met some amazing people. Two ladies in particular. Thank you so much for looking out for me that night and keeping me safe. I will forever be grateful. The opening was amazing, especially with it being my first university opening.

I met the boss over the universities and made him nervous with my militant demeanor and loud attitude. He told me I was being rough with my trainees and screaming too much. Later that day, the university executives told my boss they loved me and wanted to know if I could stay. He came to me and said, "Well, look here, kiddo, looks like you're my new grill trainer."

I looked at him and smiled. In my heart I knew I was getting closer to that number one spot. People were getting promoted left and right. Again, the plan was in full effect and I was focused.

Goals Completed

279. Wake up on the beach

61. Walk in Louisiana

First things first. May is my birthday month—that's all the positivity you need right there. I traveled to Florida from Georgia and celebrated my birthday on Panama City Beach with my grandmother and mother. Then I was put on a plane four days later headed to Nashville, Tennessee. I was there for three weeks assisting restaurants that needed help. I ended May with a trip to New Orleans with my dad and baby brother. I put on a few extra pounds in May and met some really great people, one of whom was Ms. Albany. She immediately became another mentor and encouraged me to make major changes in my life. When I left New Orleans, she challenged me to complete twenty-one goals in the month of June. I accepted her challenge and went back home. I knocked my goals out of the park.

Side note: I spent the night with Ms. Cleveland. I popped my *ATTENTION* bubble, and it was everything.

I know who I am I know what I believe, and that's all I need to know

-Will Smith

Goals Completed

84. Read five new books

9. No cigarettes for 7 Days straight

91. Complete 100 squats

82. Complete 500 squats

108 Complete 25 push-ups

109. Complete 50 push-ups

110. Complete 75 push-ups

111. Complete 100 push-ups

112. Complete 200 push-ups

257. Turn a negative into a positive

42. No cigarettes for 15 days

88. Complete shift leader book

224. No bread for 7 days

272 No pressure for 7 days

103 No alcohol for 7 days

214 No pork for 7 days

294 No beef for 7 days

229 NO white carbs for 7 days

271 Go on a hike

299 Learn the cup song

219 NO soda for 7 Days

287 Complete 100 Jumping Jacks

288 Complete 250 Jumping Jacks

295 NO beef for 15 Days

215 NO Pork for 15 days

220. No Soda for 15 days

147. Complete 250 Flutter kicks

113. Complete 350 Push ups

68. Complete 15 miles

300. Complete a Fundraiser

101. No cigarettes for 30 days

225. No bread for 15 days

*Mini Challenge for Month: Give bags to Kids for School.

June was a great month for me. Coming home and spending time with my family was what I needed. My little cousin, my heartbeat, was glued to my hip when I was home. The majority of the goals that I completed were with his help. He also challenged me this month to complete ten goals. He doesn't know how much I appreciate him, but one day I will be able to fully show how grateful I am.

I also met a new love interest. Ms. North Florida. She swiped right into my heart, and was incredible. It was a breath of fresh air to have someone who genuinely cared about me and what I had going on. I needed the attention, and she gave it effortlessly. She cooked my favorite meals, she stroked my ego, she was kind, and the sex was great.

I spent some of June in San Jose, California, with my brothers opening another university. I trained grill, and they were flawless. We even did the mannequin challenge, and it was the coolest thing ever. The people at the university were kind to us and fed us every day. I put on 10 more pounds. The trip to San Jose was truly amazing, but the best part of June was coming home to Ms. North Florida.

Don't trap yourself with the desire of wanting to be liked

-Jada Pinkett Smith

Goals Completed

234. Train Grill Five times at a New Restaurant Opening

76. Do Karaoke in Five new states

July started out emotional for me. For some reason I wanted to grow my hair, and the process made me a little depressed. When I saw the bubble appear I threw the comb at it. I had come too far to be depressed about anything. My map expanded that month to Reno, Nevada, where I had another store opening. Not my best opening, or trip for that matter, but having my brothers there with me made up for that. I honestly just wanted to come home to Ms. North Florida. I was having a hair crisis, and this was a classic restaurant this time, so that meant more food. I wasn't ready for the opening at all.

During opening day, I got beat up by every station in the restaurant. There was no one to blame but myself for not being prepared. The only positive was that I reflected and adjusted. Which meant I got better.

Later that month, for my next assignment they sent me to Bowling Green, Ohio, for another opening. It was another university with my brothers. The team was outstanding, and they caught on super quick. I trained grill, of course, and they ended up putting my picture up above the grill. I was proud of how fast they got the technique, and the team loved me and my style.

Burdened with the decision about where I wanted to live and having to make that decision fast caused me to not be as focused in this opening either. Before I left for the assignment I asked my boss at my home store if she would be willing to promote me and she said no. I took that as a sign that my time was up in Valdosta, Georgia. It was truly time to climb out of the bucket and leave the crabs where they lay.

Two cities down from Bowling Green was a casino where the boys went and played. They were having a blast without me. I wasn't as social this trip with everything going on, so I didn't blame them. I was relaxing in my hotel room when I decided to call Ms. Cleveland.

"Hello, how are you?" I asked when she answered. I hadn't talked to her in a couple of months, and I wanted to know if she still wanted me to be the godmother to her child, who was due soon. The entire conversation went left.

"How do you think it made me feel to get on social media and see you with a whole new family?" she said.

She sounded so sad, and I wasn't accustomed to her sounding this way.

"I am truly sorry," I stated with an apologetic heart. I did not know she felt this way. Did this mean she still loves me?

"You said we were going to be a family back in May. May, Moe. You said you would be at my baby shower. Now you have a family to worry about."

I had tears in my eyes because I loved her and she sounded hurt. "She knows about you, though. She said she understands my obligation to my godchild." Ms. North Florida was like that. Her heart was so pure.

Interrupting my daydream, Ms. Cleveland said clearly, "She's not coming around my child, Moe. Oh, what? You thought we would be one big happy family? Nigga, you crazy."

The next day I broke up with Ms. North Florida. No matter how much pain Ms. Cleveland had put me through, I guess I just wanted one more ride on the crazy train. I knew I broke Ms. North Florida's heart, but it was best I cut it off when I did instead of continuing something with her when I wanted to be somewhere else.

I wanted Ms. North Florida in my life, I really did, but there was a certain part of me that wanted Ms. Cleveland more.

Current Reading: 39%

Goals Completed

168. Walk in Washington DC

17. Travel by train state to state

548. Visit the Washington Monument

125. Travel to another Country

141. Do the Mexico song in Mexico

118. Become a lead

  This entire month was positive. My goddaughter was born towards the end of the month. I went outside the country for the first time, and I also added new states to my map: Arizona, Virginia, and Washington, DC. The month was filled with so much good energy. I became a Latina. Her name is La Vita, and I danced with three of the most handsome men on the team. I had the time of my life completing my goals. I also spoke to Ms. North Florida a few times, but she was done with me. I am sure she knew what was really going on even though I didn't have the heart to tell her.

  I opened two restaurants this month, and I trained grill at both. The first one was in Tucson, Arizona. It was then I became a Latina and took a trip to Mexico. I was terrified the entire time, but my brother accompanied me and made me feel a little safer. He was fluent in Spanish and communicated with everyone. I had a blast. The university wasn't set up when we got there. However, we adjusted as we always do and had a great opening. During my time in Arizona, I had the pleasure of speaking to my old best friend. Remember the one that kicked me out? She now lives with her parents, she suffers from PTSD, and is pregnant. She looked a mess when I spoke to her on video chat, but what you put out is what is returned. Karma.

I flew straight to Washington, DC, from Tucson, Arizona. The opening was another university in Fairfax, Virginia. During my stay, I met Ms. Washington. She was hood. I was hesitant to pull up in her neighborhood, but in my heart, I felt safe and turned on by her roughness. She had a boyfriend but didn't mind entertaining me and giving me what I needed while I was there. My team and I took a tour around the city. We went to the capital, to the Washington monument, museums, and we took great pictures.

The opening was laid back, and I ate a lot of pizza. I was the lead in Virginia, and I learned from being in that position that I knew nothing about setting up a restaurant. I was so happy for the opportunity, though. I made a promise to myself to do better.

In the middle of this month I found somewhere to live in Atlanta. You wouldn't believe that my new place was 4.2 miles away from Ms. Cleveland's home. Yes, I had it that bad. Regardless of the situation, that was my nigga, and I needed her to know I had her back. I was prepared to be the best godmother ever. I wanted her to see how good I was doing in life and that I wasn't a screw-up. My money was steady, and I could handle the bubbles. For the first time in a long time, I was living a life where I didn't have to depend on anyone but me.

I'm going to use all my tools, my God-Given ability, and make the best life I can with it

-Lebron James

Goals Completed

39. Move back to Atlanta

117. Become an Operations Supervisor

> *Mini Challenge for Month: Donate blood.*
> *Blood Type: O Negative*

Moving back to Atlanta was bittersweet. I was happy with the process, but my pockets were emptied. My home was beautiful, and my request was simple. I asked for a one bedroom, one bath, somewhere safe to put my car when I was traveling, washer and dryer connections, and space. A lot of it. While sitting on the floor in my living room at my new place, Monroe walked in from the garage, which was closed. She looked slightly happy to see me. "How are you, Monichia?" She stepped closer. I then saw the concern in her face, still so pretty. She wore a long, yellow dress that flowed past her legs onto the floor with diamond sandals.

I sat up and embraced her beauty as she came closer. "I'm fine," I answered with a half-smile.

"You sure? There's a lot of bubbles floating around."

I glanced around my living room. I had no idea what she was talking about. I only saw a few bubbles, and they had been around since I was in Valdosta. Monroe sat down beside me on the floor. "Why are you here, Monichia? Please tell me you are not here for her."

I got up and walked away. One thing she wasn't going to do was talk about my friend in any way other than what she deserved.

"Well, that answers that question. You are aware that I have been digging since January, right?"

I looked back at her sitting on the floor. "Do you want a cookie?"

Monroe laughed. ", that's okay, but I want you to wake up and see this woman doesn't love you the way you love her. She is using you, Monichia."

I put my hands in the air. "For what? She has everything she needs, and I have nothing to give her. And we are friends. That's it."

I sat down on the other side of my empty living room floor. "Why can't you just be happy for me? Look at my home. I went from nothing, to only having a bed and bath to now having 1,000 square feet. I have a garage, Monroe. A damn garage. Please be happy for me."

Monroe tilted her head as she looked at me. "Be happy for your damn self. Why can't you just be alone and get your shit together like everyone else, Monichia? Why do you want to be with a woman who doesn't care about you? A woman who does things to you when you're sleeping."

Confused, I asked, "What are you talking about, Monroe?"

She looked at me with the saddest eyes. "I was there at the big house with you two. I watched as you passed out drunk, and I watched her take things where they didn't belong. Why do you feel like you have to be there for someone who slept with a man the same night you proposed to her?"

I was growing frustrated with the conversation. "Why are you bringing this up now, Monroe?" I asked.

"Because it looks like you forgot," she shot back quickly. "Did you forget when she left you in the apartment because she didn't want to help you pay rent? And you must have forgotten when she told you out of her own mouth that she wanted to just get high and not pay any bills. Please explain how this time will be different."

I yelled, "It's different because we are friends. She has her place, and I have mine. I have my life and a job, and I can afford to handle any bubbles. I'm in control."

I saw Monroe glance up at my battery meter and shake her head. "Of what, Monichia? You can't allow someone to come in and get you completely sidetracked from your destiny."

Angrily I screamed, "What destiny? You won't even tell me what it is!"

Calmly Monroe stated, "Your energy is at the top of the priority list, and now you are sacrificing it for someone you think loves you."

I looked in her face. "If that's how you feel, then…"

Monroe smiled and said, "You are special, Monichia. You truly are, but you will have to pay for what you did to both women."

"Who? What women? Ms. North Florida?"

"Yes, you broke up with her while she was at work and you had no regard for her feelings. Trust me, you're gonna feel that, and it's going to hurt you twice as bad because she didn't deserve it."

I put my head in my hands. I didn't want to hear any of this. "It was three weeks, Monroe."

"And she genuinely loved you through each day of it, and you left her for a woman who we both know runs out on you when things get rough. Let's also not forget you promised Ms. Cleveland a happy ending. How are you going to promise someone a family and end up on social media with another family? It's going to be really, really bad, baby, but—"

I stood up. "I think it's time for you to go."

Monroe rolled her eyes and glanced at my battery a second time. She shook her head as she walked out the front door.

I couldn't let her get me down. I had just got a promotion at work, and things were looking up for me. My decision felt like the right one. If Karma was coming to get me, then so be it. I will deal with what happens when it happens.

Every Woman is a Queen, and we all
have different things to offer
-Queen Latifah

Goals Completed

257. Put $50 into my Savings

258. Put $100 into my savings

*Mini Challenge: Give away five jackets.

I had to work at my home store until the end of the month. Between moving and my promotion, I had to come off the road. In that time, I had been spending my days with Ms. Cleveland and my godchild. At that point, it wasn't even about Ms. Cleveland. I felt like God knew all the bad things she did, and decided to give the world something different. She was an amazing mom, and I was learning every step of the way. I had my place, a new promotion, a new beautiful baby, and my best friend. I was positive and meeting great people in the process.

Ms. Milwaukee was my soldier, again, when I needed *ATTENTION*. I felt like Ms. Cleveland might have thought I wanted to replace her with Ms. Milwaukee looking how she did before the baby and 10 years younger than when I first met her. I decided we should all be together, and it worked. I had Ms. Cleveland and Ms. Milwaukee. They communicated with each other without me and everything.

My next assignment was in Pearl, Mississippi. It had to be my walk or something because women were at that point flocking to me. That's when I met Ms. Jackson. She was something else, and again I needed attention. I told the ladies back home about her, and they said I could have her. Ms. Jackson accompanied me in my hotel room several nights. I held and kissed her softly. We rested in each other's arms with the plan to become a big happy family. I wanted to share her with my ladies so I was patient with her body. I truly had all the women I needed.

The opening itself was pretty cool. I had a blast opening the restaurant with my team. We had some newbies on this trip, and they were cute. I was extremely happy to be able to show them a good time, and assist with anything they needed on their first opening. October brought great things, especially my two new friends, Ms. Tallahassee and Ms. South Florida.

Ms. Tallahassee admitted to being bisexual so of course I made it a point to get her attention. She however had a boyfriend back home so we decided to just be friends. Ms. South Florida was the sweetest. She instantly became my friend. We stayed up many nights talking about life and our dreams. She was beautiful and listened to everything I had to say. She was single and not even a little bit interested in women. I learned from Monroe to stop trying to sleep with my friends. So, I embraced our friendship and looked forward to seeing it blossom. She was peaceful and kind and I needed that.

I'm pretty, but not beautiful

I Sin but I'm not the devil

I'm good, but Im not an angel

-Marilyn Monroe

Goals Completed

447. Walk in Texas

240. Raise my Credit Score 50 points

327. Learn to bowl properly

259. Put $500 into my savings

464. Train Grill 10 Times at New Restaurant Opening

198. Walk in Italy

404. Stop smoking Cigarettes for 6 months

November was an extremely long month for me. I spent part of it in Pearl, Mississippi, and the other half in Ennis, Texas. Both assignments were new store openings, and I was beat-down tired. At that point I realized all money wasn't good money, but Christmas was coming so I wouldn't complain. During my opening in Texas I took a ride with my boss. He asked me about my schedule and said I was the best one they had on the team. There it was, a year after my first assignment I had made it to that number one spot.

I spent Thanksgiving in the restaurant in Texas working. It was better to work than to be stuck in a hotel. The store had a cool setup, but it was inside a gas station. I thought it was neat until the flies took over. One flew in my ear, and I almost died twice. I couldn't wait to leave Texas and the flies. The crew was really nice to me. Some of them brought me Thanksgiving dinner. I appreciated the love, but I missed my goddaughter so much I was growing sick. I couldn't really focus at work because my heart was at home being fed her bottle. I would do anything for my princess, and her mother knew it. The positive part about this month was that my goddaughter and I had this thing where I would go "aahh," and she would go "aahh." It was the cutest conversation. Simple, yet so adorable.

I wanted to propose to Ms. Cleveland again. I even talked to her about it. We agreed on a lot of things, and she said it wouldn't be a bad idea. Taking things to the next level is what anyone would want to do, but for my goddaughter's sake, we decided to take things slow. We currently had two girlfriends, and everyone was waiting for me to get home. I was truly living the life of a king. I had my woman, my daughter, and my ladies. Everything was all good.

Goals Completed

361. Visit the Corporate Office

I was having difficulties at my home store. It was
another female boss, and we just couldn't connect. I didn't
really want to be on the road anymore, but being in my new
home store was not an option. I didn't want to leave my
goddaughter, but for my sanity I had to go.

I was sent to San Antonio, Texas, for a week to do a
preview for work. A week was a break that I really needed.
It was truly work having a new baby. We had a little
routine. After working ten hours, at night I'd go over to play
with her and hope she would go back to sleep so I could lay
down.

That week in San Antonio I turned in 80-plus hours.
I was beat, but my goddaughter's first Christmas was
approaching and I needed it to be perfect. When I got back
home, there was a snowstorm in Atlanta. One thing led to
another, and Ms. Cleveland moved in. By moving in, I mean
I took all her things down three flights of steps and put them
in my place. At any point she could've said, "No, don't
move my things," but she didn't. So, I took it to mean that

now she wanted to be serious. This was year three of the crazy train, and she was finally being nice to me.

When I received my next assignment. I didn't want to go, but the tension in my home store drove me out. Again, I made more money on the road. Now that I had a family to think about, I had to be smart with my moves. My next assignment was in Valley, Alabama, where I was training drive-thru. I missed my family so much my head hurt. I was truly distracted. My heart wasn't in training or in Alabama. During the first week, an incident happened and I had to leave work. I was being sent home.

I was in my hotel room praying to God that he would remove all the bubbles and make room for more positives in the upcoming year. My request was simple. I asked that he remove anything in my life that was a liability to my success. I heard the bathroom door open, and it was Monroe. She had on dark blue jeans, a white blouse, and some all-white Keds. She looked stunning and relaxed. She sat down in the chair beside the TV.

"Are you dumb or just stupid, Monichia? When was the last time you looked at your battery meter?"

I said I didn't know, but the truth was that I hadn't looked at it since March, and I was too afraid to look at it now. Why was Monroe so upset? Was she jealous?

"You do realize I've been digging since January, right?"

Confused, I asked, "Why do you keep reminding me?"

"Monichia, she doesn't want you. She is going to leave you. She's done it three times before. You have to get her out of your house."

I stepped closer to Monroe and looked her in the eyes. "We are happy. My mother is coming up for Christmas and everything. We are going to be a family, Monroe."

She stared back at me, unblinking. "If you end this now, we still have a chance. You clearly have lost your mind. What about your destiny? Are you going to give up on it?"

Irritated, I sat on the bed. "You won't even tell me what it is. So, miss me with this conversation."

"You're not being positive, Monichia," Monroe said, raising her hands.

"I am, though. I'm being positive because I'm calmly talking to a person who doesn't exist. Why aren't you down there digging, Monroe? I'm getting so sick of you just popping up trying to control my life. I love her, Monroe. And if I have to give up on my destiny, then so be it. I don't understand why I can't do both—have my destiny and have my love."

Monroe smiled. "One, because she doesn't love you."

I rolled my eyes.

"You are one of the chosen ones, Monichia. You can't give up. Whether you like it or not, you were put here for one thing."

I rolled my eyes again.

"For what, Monroe?" I asked.

"To change the world, Monichia. You were born with the gift of healing. Your heart is so pure and forgiving because it heals itself. It allows you to love like you've never been hurt before. Unconditionally to all. She is going to leave you, Monichia. Not because of anything you did, but because she isn't a part of your journey. You are powerful, and you were put here to inspire people. Your voice has to be heard, but it drowns in your love for her. You love her and her daughter more than you love yourself. So right now, she holds all your power. You lost control today at work. Why? Because your mind was on her. Where it doesn't belong. Right now, she has your mind, body, heart, and soul. And when she departs, you will fall. And it won't be to the bottom. The bottom is gone, Monichia. You will fall to the place where I stopped digging."

I looked at Monroe.

"If you fall, Monichia, you will go straight through the bottom." She gave me a half smile and stood up. "Find that woman that was ready to change the world. She didn't know how she would do it, but that didn't stop her. She had no money to feed herself but was still feeding everyone else. Find that woman and love her. Because right now she is unloved, under-appreciated, and angry."

I watched Monroe leave my hotel room. I heard everything she said, but my mind was made up. I was going home to my future wife and my beautiful daughter, and that was that.

The truth is, everyone is going to hurt you You just got to find the ones worth suffering for

-Bob Marley

Under our tree glittered 137 presents. I must say I outdid myself. I got Ms. Cleveland everything on her list plus more. Between all the gifts, decorations, bills, food, and living, I had spent $3,000 in one week. Two days ago my car broke down. I was so nervous when it happened because I didn't want Ms. Cleveland to feel like I couldn't hold my weight. I wanted her to know I could support her. However, she was calm. She told my mother when she left yesterday that she had my back, and I believed her. This time we would be okay. Regardless of what anyone thought, she had changed and I was her witness. We were a family, and Christmas 2017 was the best Christmas ever.

You've got to learn to leave the table
when love's no longer being served
-Nina Simone

Ms. Cleveland drove me to work that evening. That was the last time I rode in her car.

You can close your eyes to the things
you don't want to see But you can't
close your heart to things you don't
want to feel
-Johnny Depp

I took a taxi to work. Ms. Cleveland had somewhere to be. She said she couldn't take me. I pouted, but of course I called my ride. It was $30 to get to work, and $30 to get home.

I believe in breaking up with bad
friends too.
-Wendy Williams

The excuse today was that it was too much to get our daughter up and ready to take me twenty minutes down the interstate. I walked out the door, while she laid on the couch watching TV. I came home from work fourteen hours later, and she was laying in same spot sleeping peacefully. I wanted her to know everything would be okay. To have faith in me. Believe in me. This car thing wouldn't hold me down.

Life is sometimes hard and you have to
laugh your way through it
-Madea

She watched me get ready for work, call my ride, wait for my ride, kiss my daughter, walk out the door, and get in the car. She waited twenty minutes, and then she texted me. They were leaving. She knew I couldn't come back home. I couldn't afford to. Poisoned in anger, I felt like being hit by a car.

Turn your wounds into Wisdom

-Oprah Winfrey

I finished off a bottle of vodka and tripped over two bubbles. Ms. Chicago was headed my way. She thought I wanted her to take me to run errands, but really, I just wanted a hug. I needed one. I was in so much pain that I felt nothing. I returned what gifts I gave Ms. Cleveland for Christmas that I could. Rent was paid, I had groceries, but I still needed to get to work. I was heartbroken, but I had to maintain. Ms. South Florida was coaching me through the entire process. Every time I called her, she answered, and it didn't matter where she was. I appreciated her friendship, and I'll forever be grateful. Ironically, after all that, I didn't fall through the bottom. I'm stronger than Monroe thought.

I believe if you'll just stand up and go

life will open up for you

-Tina Turner

I returned home to Valdosta, Georgia. Once again, my mother had to save me. She gave me her spare car and helped me back on my feet. I can't imagine my life without her. One day I hope to repay her for every time she cleared her savings for me. The times she healed me and I would leave patched again, only to return later, broken by another woman. I wanted my mother to be proud of me. I wanted her to see me successful and not in need of anything but love.

I sat down on my sofa with a glass of Crown and Coke. I was finally able to purchase my Royal. Relaxed I got on social media and scrolled through to find some entertainment. One thing led to another, and I ended up on Ms. Cleveland's page. To my surprise, she had gotten engaged to a man two days prior.

She waited a whole damn week. As I fell through the bottom, I saw Ms. North Florida's face on the way down. I rolled my eyes because I knew that I was getting the same energy I had put out into the universe. Clearly Monroe had been digging for a long time because once I landed I was completely exhausted from falling. When I rolled over, Monroe was looking at me and holding a cup of tea. She wore pinstriped pants with some badass black pumps and a black blouse. She was expecting me. I rolled my eyes again.

"Are you ready to fulfill your destiny?"

"Not really. I need to get back up there. I don't belong here, Monroe." I looked up at Monroe with a sad face.

"You have to heal, or you will make the same mistake. We have to remove those bubbles you have everywhere. You need time."

"I'm good, I swear. I'm not stressing over any hoe or any bubbles. I have some wheels now, I still got money in the bank, I'm getting sent to another store, and I'm okay. I promise."

I left Monroe sitting there with her tea and ended up at Ms. Cleveland's front door five days later. When she opened the door, she handed me the remaining things of mine she still had. I forced my way into her house and went straight to the bedroom. My goddaughter was up. I honestly didn't even want to talk to Ms. Cleveland. I really just wanted to play with my princess. Ms. Cleveland picked my goddaughter up and went and put her in her car seat. I went and sat on the couch and crossed my legs.

I wasn't hurting at that point to where I was livid, but I wanted to fight. My face had been the destination for her fist on many occasions, and it was my turn to return the favor. She grabbed a knife out of the kitchen and her phone.

I watched her closely as she put the phone to her ear.

"Yes, ma'am, I have an intruder. My daughter's here. The neighbors are on their way. Please, come help me."

Calmly I took out my phone and dialed 911. I put them on speaker.

"911, what's your emergency?"

"Yes, my girlfriend is on the phone with you guys saying there is an intruder, but it's only me. She is also standing in front of me holding a knife."

She then ran to me, showing me her phone.

"I was only playing, Moe. What are you doing?"

"Clearly, I'm not playing with you, bitch!" I screamed.

"Get out of my house. Please, Moe, just get out of my house." She looked so irritated.

"I just want to talk."

"I don't want to talk to you, Moe. I don't even want you here," she said, packing the baby's bag.

"Let's talk about your new husband. How is it fucking possible for you to go get a man to marry you in a week? I'm so confused. Please help me figure out this mystery."

"Moe, leave my house!" She took my goddaughter outside and was gone for about six minutes. I scanned my surroundings quickly. I knew Ms. Cleveland had a gun, but to be honest I came there ready to die if it came to that. I wanted a fair fight, and I wasn't leaving until she gave it to me. When she returned, my phone rung. It was my mother. I ignored the call.

"Welcome back, champ."

"Moe, get out of my house. I don't want you or want you here."

"So, you can't fight anymore. You only hit me when you know I won't hit you back. Where is that big tough bitch I know? Where you at, Ohio? Hit me. You had me out here spending money on you and you got a whole dude. You think it's cool to be playing with people and their feelings?"

After the third unanswered called from my mother, I picked up.

"Hello."

"Leave, Monichia, please. She is going to call the police." She sounded so scared.

"No, she won't, momma. It smells like weed in here. She doesn't want the police here. They will take our princess away."

"MONICHIA, SHE DOESN'T WANT YOU! Leave now. You have come too far to throw everything away."

I looked at Ms. Cleveland. Why did she call my momma?

"She can't keep hurting me, momma. I can't let her do that." I yelled into my phone.

"Leave, baby. It's not worth it." I could hear my mother's heart racing through the phone.

"I just want to fight, momma. She's been beating me down for so long, and now she doesn't want to fight."

"Baby, no. It's not worth it." She sounded so pitiful.

I hung up in my mother's face and stood up. I looked Ms. Cleveland in the eyes.

"You're gonna have to whoop my ass today, bitch, cause I'm not leaving. You're gonna take my daughter from me and go be with some man? You're just gonna have her around some random ass person?"

She looked shocked and a little proud that I was finally starting to stand up to her.

"Moe, if you cared at all you wouldn't have let me take her out of here. She's out there in the cold. Please, just leave."

My mother called twice more before Monroe appeared. She had on a white gown, pink furry slippers, and a pink bonnet. She did not have on jewelry or makeup, and her skin shined in the dark apartment. She was gorgeous, but she was pissed!

"You're doing way too much. You should've hit that hoe and left. Now you're just emotional, screaming, and looking like a damn fool. Girl, answer that phone and go home."

I answered my mother's call.

"Monichia, please, baby, it's the day before my birthday. Please don't do this. Don't hurt your momma like this. Please, baby, go home."

I listened.

Walking out the door, I knew in my heart I would never see Ms. Cleveland or my goddaughter again. I wanted her to know that I loved her and I was happy for her. I knew she had wanted a husband and a family. That wasn't the point at all. The point was I was her friend. I should've known about him from the beginning. She had asked me to cut off our girlfriends because she became jealous. Just to leave me.

I wanted to say, "I love you and send me an invitation to the wedding." I wanted her to know I couldn't wait to show up wearing some badass heels. Instead I told her he would never marry her. I screamed that she was a hoe and always would be. Truth is, I wanted her to marry me, not him. I got in my car, and that was the last time I saw Ms. Cleveland.

I called Ms. South Florida when I got home and cried to her. She knew how hurt I was and didn't judge me for crying. We video-chatted the entire night, and she helped me deal with my reality.

I ended January with Ms. Canton and Ms. Brooklyn. I met Ms. Canton during my transition to another home store, and Ms. Brooklyn online. I was in need of attention, and they both provided.

You can't live life looking at yourself
from someone else point of view
-Penelope Cruz

Goals Completed

24. Complete 15 Openings with My Wings

326. Learn to shoot pool properly

In mid-February I found myself falling back through the bottom. This time it was behind Ms. Brooklyn. Of course, I needed *ATTENTION*. She gave it to me and took everything I had in the process. I had to make a decision between her and Ms. Canton because my heart wouldn't allow me to deal with both. Ms. Canton was fresh air. Loyal by default but I didn't choose her. I chose Ms. Brooklyn. She was too fly. The way she dressed, her accent, everything about her had me feeling better about my self-esteem.

I fell through when I was on an assignment in Jacksonville, North Carolina. Ms. Brooklyn whispered pages of sweet-nothings, and I believed every word. I needed to feel wanted, and I felt like she wanted me, so I was wrapped around her finger. After her BMW got totaled, she spent several nights at my home because I was her ride to work. I didn't even have my own car, so being someone else's ride to work was hysterical. She said she loved me, and that was enough to give her the keys to my home, my mother's car, and my heart.

Once I left for my assignment, everything changed. She no longer answered the phone when I called; however, she had my mother's car and my house keys. She was cold when I finally reached her and she acted as if I was disturbing her. When her entire family turned their back on her, I stepped in like a fool and financed her struggle.

When I landed after my fall, Monroe looked disgusted. But when she felt the pain I was in, she became gentle. I told her everything and begged her to fix it. Ms. Chicago and Ms. Canton went and got my mother's car and my house keys from Ms. Brooklyn's workplace. I was too embarrassed, but I needed my things.

I was so hurt by the way Ms. Brooklyn treated me that I became depressed during my assignment. My team did the best they could to support me, but I knew this still was Karma from Ms. North Florida. I spent a few nights with Monroe working on my heart and a plan to fix my pain. She encouraged me to start building my company. She said when I thought about Ms. Brooklyn to start writing. I did and ended up completing two business plans. The pain fueled my grind. I was angry, I was tired, but I was focused on my destiny

Goals Completed

547. Visit the Gateway Arch

154. Visit three new museums

406. Build a Bear to cuddle with

689. Take a picture on the roof of a Restaurant

159. Attend the circus for first time.

160. Attend Universal Soul Circus

173. Become a salaried manager

77. Complete karaoke in 10 states

45. Lose 50 lbs.

567. Learn to make Collard Greens

As soon as I landed in Atlanta, Ms. Chicago came to my immediate attention. We went to see a black superhero movie, and she took me to the circus. I wondered if I could make a request to send Ms. Chicago a great Christian man. My best friend deserved it. I know as long as she was breathing I would be straight up here in Atlanta. It's rare to find that in friends. Ms. Chicago prayed for me, and with me. Along with everything else, she had my back in the restaurant industry. We laughed about how Ms. Brooklyn stole her juice. It made me realize that she was desperate and petty because she took several things from my home as well. I was excited about the thought that I could actually learn from her. Of course, there was nothing that I really wanted her to show me. She was cold and mean and did not deserve to be in my life. I had only been dealing with her for three weeks, and it made me realize that I was still paying for Ms. North Florida. She too had spent a few hundred on me during our encounter and I was cold to her later. So, I expected not to get the money back that Ms. Brooklyn owed me.

I asked Monroe if Karma was done with me when she came to see me one Sunday evening. She had on a Lakers jersey with denim shorts, and some high-top sneakers with a baseball cap. As usual, she was gorgeous. She replied, "Yes, love, you have been through enough."

I got up and walked to the kitchen to fix a glass of juice when Monroe asked, "When is the last time you went to the doctor?"

"Doctor for what?" I asked, confused.

"The woman's doctor." Monroe looked at me with concern. "You have so many wires in your sexual tube . . . we have to get that thang checked out."

We laughed. "I'll schedule an appointment in the morning."

To change the subject, I let her know I was going after my goals. I needed to know if I started making requests would I be denied because of my past mistakes.

Monroe stated, "Just keep being positive, and make your requests. What's meant for you is yours, and I believe your stars have aligned."

Curiously I asked, "What do you mean?"

"What numbers have you been seeing?"

"The number one. I see 11:11 or 1:11 on the clock every day. Or I see it on street signs, tag numbers, or buildings. It's kinda creepy because I see it like three times a day."

Monroe smiled but stayed silent.

"I should've played them."

"You really should play with them in real life."

"I'm confused," I said while scratching my head.

"You're one of the chosen ones, Monichia. Touched by an anointing that only the strong can handle. You have no choice but to be great in real life. Not just in your head, or on social media, or in these restaurants. It's time for you to be great in real life. Invest in Monichia. Love Monichia. So now, what's your request?"

"Will you send me my First Lady?"

"Your what? Monichia, haven't you had enough ladies? My goodness."

"Yes, but now please send me the one. Chocolate, and from the South, please. Clearly Northern girls and I don't mix well. Not a country girl like me, though, but still from the South. Whatever she is lacking, let me make up for it; and whatever I'm lacking, let her make up for it."

"Why won't you just focus on your goals so you won't be lacking and meet someone who is secured as well? You need time."

"No, I need my First Lady. She has to be a hustler but good with kids, but she doesn't have any kids herself yet. She has to want to motivate our youth with me. I need her to love me and only me. She has—"

Monroe interrupted. "So, are we really in here building a woman? I'm not. I refuse." She laughed and threw up her hands.

"It's my request, though! You just said I'm the chosen one."

"One of the chosen ones, I clearly said."

"Well, that's still fly in itself. So, I need something to hold this greatest at night. She has to be nasty, too!"

"Monichia." Monroe stood up.

I looked at her. "What? You see that *ATTENTION* bubble. It comes twice a day sometimes. I haven't a choice in that part of my life, so I'm asking for your help. Send her to me, and I will not fuck this up. She also needs a car. Because I'm still driving my mother's car."

"What else?"

"I get one more request?" I asked excitedly.

"Yes, but then you have to go put more positivity out there."

"Okay, well, I can't start Finesse on the road. I have to stop traveling in order to get my boots in order."

Monroe smiled and walked towards the front door. "Keep describing the woman you want every day until you feel butterflies."

"What?"

She blew me a kiss and closed the door.

The next day I walked into work, and the boss sat me down. He wrote a number on a piece of paper, slid it to me, and said he wanted me off the road and in his store as a salaried manager. I looked down at the numbers and couldn't refuse. At that moment, I was a believer. I was ready to fulfill my purpose. No more looking back. No more falling. Just elevation.

I decided to take one more trip and make the last one my best one. Go out with a bang. They sent me to train grill in Litchfield, Illinois. My roommate this time was Ms. South Florida. She told me previously I was her best friend. I felt that the title fit because we had spoken every other day, if not every day since Christmas. She had witnessed a couple breakdowns and made me laugh through them all. She knew about all my women. Up to the current date she knew every city and state. She wanted Ms. Cleveland's head and had no respect for Ms. Brooklyn.

She never made any judgments toward me. She remained kind and gentle throughout my healing process. Ms. South Florida was a straight woman who graduated from FAMU. She had been in the restaurant industry for over ten years, but she wanted to be a high school guidance counselor. I was happy to have her as my roommate on my final trip. I hadn't seen her in person since November of 2017, so I knew we would turn up for our cities.

When I landed, the team was already there. Once I arrived at the restaurant, I felt good about life. I had removed several bubbles, and things were looking up. I was seeing 1s more and more, and embracing everything coming. With this being my last opening, it has to be the best one.

I saw Ms. South Florida before she saw me. When she came to greet me, her hug was the sweetest. It felt good to embrace her. Her words were in constant rotation in the mental tube to where her wire budded out into my emotional tube. She was an amazing friend, and I was grateful.

When she walked away from me, the butterflies came. I was sure this was a mistake. Because she was straight, and never gave me the notion she wanted me to try her. But I wasn't going to argue with the universe. The butterflies were present, and I was ready to change her life.

March 23rd is our anniversary.

**Be the change you wish to see in the
world
-Mahatma Gandi**

Goals Completed

181. Become a Certified Training Manager

57. Complete Lawn Service Business Plan

58. Complete Cleaning Service Business Plan

444. Obtain Cleaning Service License

460. Obtain Lawn Service License

I wanted to live a life where I didn't have to depend on anyone but myself. I am truly happy to say I've completed the original mission, and have upgraded to a new plan with a bigger objective. I've always wanted to change the world; however, I had to save myself from destruction to be able to save anyone else. It was never truly about me. I wasn't striving for The Forbes List. I wanted to be in the history books. I wanted to be listed with the greats. I believe in my heart I'm ready for this movement. At this point I'm just waiting for my marching orders. I took the promotion, and I haven't traveled anywhere new. I had been in my home store for two weeks, and I was not happy about it. The promotion was awesome, but the store was depressing. The majority of the stores were. No one really cared or had the same pride we had when we opened new restaurants.

I wanted to inspire millions, and that is what would happen. I wasn't going to allow myself to get caught in the chains of the company. I had a destiny to fulfill. So being unhappy at work wasn't happening. It had only been two weeks since I got the promotion, but I refused to be somewhere where I'm not happy. My request was simple. Get me off of my home store schedule without losing my salaried pay. I wasn't sure if the request had been made because I hadn't seen Monroe. I wasn't sure if I had built up enough positivity to make the request. I had only been in my new position for two weeks, but I had to get off their schedule. So, if I had to do some extra positive things to make up for some Karma, I did whatever I could.

Four days after my request, my boss pulled me to the side and asked how I felt about training managers. I laughed in my mind because I barely knew how to be a manager. But I did know how to make people happy. If that meant being quick on the grill, or making the kid in the dining room smile, or getting my team motivated to help me make people happy, that was what I did. The whole time he was talking I was saying thank you in my spirit. I knew there were people around me who were more qualified for the position on paper. But they didn't make the request. At that moment, I knew I had to put more positivity around me because my request was huge.

Ms. South Florida had relocated to Atlanta. I honestly don't know how I made that happen, but it needed to happen for both of us. In my mind, she was already the First Lady in my company. Because I knew this was true, there was no need for me to wait on something that's mine. She had her position, and it was past time for her to enjoy it.

I am only listening to the joy bells
ringing in my mind They have my full
permission to play over and over again
-Wanda D Hollis

Goals Completed

450. Create a yearly lesson plan for Mentoring Service

459. Create website for Finesse

461. Purchase P.O Box for Finesse

462. Get insurance for Finesse

492. Purchase cleaning chemicals for Cleaning Service

493. Purchase vacuum cleaner for Cleaning Service

494. Purchase brooms for Cleaning Service

495. Purchase mops for Cleaning Service

496. Purchase buckets for Cleaning Service

497. Purchase cleaning towels for Cleaning Service

498. Purchase long handle dust pan for Cleaning Service

520. Sign one contract for Cleaning Service

510. Purchase containers for Meal Prepping Service

448. Purchase tool box for Finesse

May, as you know, is my birth month. This year I turned 27. I didn't do much to celebrate, but I enjoyed it. Ms. South Florida got me gifts, as well as Ms. Chicago. They were both out of town during my special day, but they made sure I smiled. I spent my birthday evening with Ms. Westwood, a friend from New Jersey. We listened to music, drank a lot of wine, and ate expensive food. My birthday overall was fabulous. The remainder of the month was spent building my company. I didn't sleep at all. I had one shot to get this movement together. So the First Lady and I went into training because I had no idea how to start a cleaning service. I followed my business plan step by step.

I reached out to people in my community and asked if we could clean their homes for free. Of course, they said yes. We learned the skill, the technique, and the pricing. At the end of the month, we received a call from a body shop who wanted our services. It was our first contract, and receiving it while still in training was huge. I hadn't seen Monroe, but I was making good moves. I knew when she did appear I would be ready to receive my orders.

Goals Completed

374. Take a cruise for first time

140. Walk on an Island

Two years ago, I ended the month of June unable to pay my rent. Now, I am on a cruise ship in the Bahamas, and the difference in my life is completely blowing my mind.

It was 3:00 a.m., and the ship was silent. I was tipsy and stretched out on the deck. When I glanced to my left, I saw Monroe coming towards me in a yellow swimsuit with a matching cover-up and strappy, heeled sandals. She always looked so pretty in yellow. "Monroe!" I screamed, happy to see her.

"How are you?" She strutted towards me with a smile that made my heart warm.

"I'm fabulous. Can you believe this boat?" I got up and pointed over the rail. "Look at this water. It's so beautiful."

I glanced back at Monroe. She was silent, but looked like she had something on her mind.

"What's wrong? What did I do now?"

She smiled. "You're doing everything right, Monichia. However, I'm sad to say I won't be digging for you anymore." Monroe sat down and looked at me.

"Why? Are you leaving me again?" My eyes started to tear up.

"It's time for you to dig for yourself." Monroe sat back in her chair, crossing her legs.

"What if I don't want to dig?" I asked. "You're good at it. It's your thing."

"Monichia, you have to. If you don't, your mother will have to keep digging for you, and she can only do so much at this point. She's married and digging with her husband. But because she loves you, she will stop digging her own foundation to help you dig yours. When are you going to give your mother a break? Your tubes are all clear. I mean, you can do a little work in your physical tube, but overall, you're fine."

"What do you mean a little work?"

"Monichia, you lost 50 pounds, only to gain it right back."

"I've been busy, Monroe. It's not easy being awesome."

Monroe smiled. "I understand that, but you have to take care of your body. Your health has to be at its best for this to work. Have you gotten that lump checked out under your left breast?"

"I did. They said it was nothing."

"But they advised that you go to a specialist. Have you been?" Monroe smiled.

I put my head down. "No, ma'am."

"So again, your health has to be at its best for you to fulfill your destiny. What have you learned in the last two years?"

"Fuck bitches get money."

Monroe didn't laugh, but I did.

"If only that were true, Monichia. If only that were true."

I caught the shade and laughed harder.

"What else?" Monroe switched which legs she had crossed.

"I learned that anything is possible. Anything I want to be or want in life can be mine if I just work hard for it. Nothing is unreachable. I also learned that being positive is the only way to live. And that I have to close the door in my vagina that leads directly to my heart."

Monroe laughed. "Lock it, too. Put chains and a warning sign up on that thang."

I shot her a bird with a perfectly manicured middle finger and rolled my eyes.

"I learned that I can't let anyone take advantage of me."

Monroe leaned her head to the side. "Did you write that letter?"

"Yes, ma'am, it's in my wallet. You want to hear it?"

"I surely do." Monroe smiled and looked up at me with the most beautiful eyes.

I reached in my back pocket to retrieve the letter. I sat down beside Monroe and cleared my throat.

Dear Moe,

I love you. I want to start this letter by saying you're beautiful. No matter what anyone could possibly say. Remember you're beautiful and we don't need their approval for that. You are capable of anything you put your mind to. You can stop drinking, you can stop smoking, you can be successful, and you definitely can stop being a rug for people.

Get up, Moe, and be proud of the amazing woman you are. Stand up and be greater than you ever were before, and I'll stand with you. I will never leave you, Moe. I won't hurt you like those people did. I won't laugh at you. Your dreams are not funny to me. I will support you regardless of your available balance. I don't care how much you weigh or what clothes you wear. Time is the greatest gift you can give me. You don't have to buy my love. You don't have to buy my friendship. I will pick up every time you call. I will never hit you. I will never cheat.

Why? Because I know you're worth it. I know you're priceless. I love you, Moe. I will listen to your poems and stories. I'll even sit back and watch the Golden Girls *with you when you can't sleep. I'll help you write in your Goals book every day and help you achieve them! I will protect you. I will never let you get behind the wheel of a car when you're drunk. I love you too much for that.*

You can be yourself around me because I accept you for who you are. You're not weird. You're special, and I need you. I need you so much, Moe. I need you to love me because no one else does

a better job than you. No one understands me like
you do. No one sees me in a bright light but you.

     Love me, Moe. Hug me. Accept me. Believe
in me. Let your past go and close your heart to me.
We completed each other. There will never be a me
without you, or a you without me. I love you, Moe.
Please don't spend another minute without loving
me.

Sincerely,
Monichia

With tears in her eyes, Monroe said, "Congratulations, you
have officially started digging. I will always be here
watching you elevate, but this is your journey and you have
to handle it alone. I have dug enough to get you to your first
million. On your journey to it, I need you to promise that
you will take time to dig deeper into your foundation every
step of the way."

     Monroe stood up and looked down at me. "Pinky
promise."

     I repeated, "Pinky promise."

     We kissed our hands to seal the vow.

     "Oh, and before I go . . . stop texting that girl."

"What girl? What are you talking about?"

"Are you forgetful now, Monichia? You have a beautiful woman at home that is busting her ass cleaning for your cleaning service and you're out here on this beautiful boat. You can't ask for a better person to love you, Monichia. So, yeah, close and lock that door because you only need one woman in your heart, and she is it. She doesn't want to share her spot, either. She believes you are amazing and that you are enough for her for the rest of her life."

I guess I looked shocked, but it was hard to believe that the woman I had been wanting all my life was here. She was my friend, and I knew in my heart she loved me.

"Stop searching for that perfect woman you created in your mind. She doesn't exist. But what does exist is the woman at home who wants to be enough for you for the rest of your life. She will find those messages."

"I deleted them," I said.

"You think you did. But she will find them."

"I'll just tell her."

"No, just let her find them when it's her time to find them. She won't leave you, but she will be hurt."

"I'll fix it."

"You have to. I know you are in control, and I believe in you. I love you, Monichia."

With that, Monroe turned and walked away. I was **Currently Reading 68%,** and there was nothing to do but elevate. I was ready for the bubbles, knowing that with elevation comes more bubbles. Sure, some of them are hard to pop. But that won't stop me. I was ready to fulfill my destiny. This journey to 100% has so far been amazing. I am eager to reach it and even more excited to start the process of maintaining it.

Part II

The Introduction of My Mother

Nicole McCloud

27 years ago

May 1991

To Monichia
My Little Black Princess

To you I am a star

And you are by far my biggest fan

This spring in 1991

You became a part of my life plan

You see I'm only 19 and Now I'm your mommy

And it is my responsibility to teach you how to be a woman

and a lady

We will not agree on everything

But my Love for you will never change

For every step you make I'll take two

I'll be that light that shines for you.

You will receive your first instructions from me

On how to become a Proverbs 31 type Lady

You will learn how to be strong

You will learn right from wrong

You will learn after a heartbreak to move on

You will learn you were born to make mistakes

But not to scared to pave the way

You will learn sin comes from within

And not the color of your skin

You will learn you came from royalty

Not slavery

You will learn all about America

But you will love and honor Africa

You will learn as a Queen

To stand by your King And fight the Enemy

You will learn that every man you meet will not be a King

And life will bring some tragedies

You will learn that it is nice to be important

But more important to be nice.

You will learn you are what you believe

And it is okay to follow your dreams.

You will learn how to turn thoughts into reality

And with that baby girl

It's You and I against the world

And oh yes that day will come

When you will have to teach your little one

To Be Continued...

Acknowledgments

Thank you to everyone who supported me with this project.
Shirley Moore Everett, Nicole McCloud, Shiyandra Wright,
Dennis Lane Jr, Jason Reed, Frank Jones IV, Windell Beal,
Nastassia Muhammad, Laketha Tutt, Tulips Freedom,
Wanda D Hollis, Jakara Stewart, Wynter Robinson,
Mistie Johnson, Nashauna Brooks, Shemele Brown,
Noelle Brock-Coetes, Courtney Fleming, Tia Conley